American Biographies

GERONIMO

Ann Weil

Chicago, Illinois

BIOG
GER

www.capstonepub.com
Visit our website to find out more information about Heinemann-Raintree books.

To order:
☎ Phone 888-454-2279
💻 Visit www.capstonepub.com
to browse our catalog and order online.

Edited by Abby Colich, Megan Cotugno, and Laura Hensley
Designed by Cynthia Della-Rovere
Original illustrations © Capstone Global Library Limited 2011
Illustrated by Oxford Designers & Illustrators
Picture research by Tracy Cummins
Originated by Capstone Global Library Limited
Printed and bound in China by Leo Paper Group

16 15 14 13 12
10 9 8 7 6 5 4 3 2 1

Library of Congress Cataloging-in-Publication Data
Weil, Ann.
  Geronimo / Ann Weil.
    p. cm.—(American biographies)
  Includes bibliographical references and index.
  ISBN 978-1-4329-6447-4 (hb)—ISBN 978-1-4329-6458-0 (pb) 1. Geronimo, 1829-1909. 2. Apache Indians—Kings and rulers—Biography. 3. Apache Indians—Wars, 1883-1886. I. Title.
  E99.A6W376 2011
  979.004'97250092—dc23   2011037571
  [B]

Acknowledgments
The author and publishers are grateful to the following for permission to reproduce copyright material: Corbis: pp. 7 (© CORBIS), 15 (© CORBIS), 16 (© Bettmann), 22 (© CORBIS), 36 (© Bettmann), 38 (© CORBIS), 41 (© Tim Thompson); Getty Images: pp. 13 (Camillus S. Fly/MPI), 19 (MPI), 23 (Time Life Pictures/US Signal Corps), 27 (PhotoQuest), 33 (Time Life Pictures/US Signal Corps), 37 (Fotosearch); Library of Congress Prints and Photographs: pp. 5, 9, 10, 11, 12, 21, 24, 28, 29, 31, 35, 39, 40; Shutterstock: p. 8 (© Nathan Chor); The Granger Collection, NYC: pp. 17, 25.

Cover photograph of "Geronimo" wearing headdress, photographed by Warren Mack Oliver, reproduced with permission from the Library of Congress Prints and Photographs.

Every effort has been made to contact copyright holders of material reproduced in this book. Any omissions will be rectified in subsequent printings if notice is given to the publisher.

Disclaimer
All the Internet addresses (URLs) given in this book were valid at the time of going to press. However, due to the dynamic nature of the Internet, some addresses may have changed, or sites may have changed or ceased to exist since publication. While the author and publisher regret any inconvenience this may cause readers, no responsibility for any such changes can be accepted by either the author or the publisher.

Contents

Some words are shown in bold, **like this**.
These words are explained in the glossary.

An Apache Warrior

By 1886 the United States had forced almost every American Indian onto a **reservation**. But in the Southwest, fewer than 40 Apache men, women, and children still fought back. The U.S. government sent 5,000 soldiers to capture them. But the army was really after only one man. His name was Geronimo.

Geronimo was an Apache warrior. He led other Apache warriors in battles against their enemies. White settlers were terrified of him. To them he was a heartless killer who would murder entire families, even unarmed women and children. Geronimo's own people saw a different man. To them he was a **medicine man** with special god-given powers.

Renegade

Geronimo fought against U.S. Army troops so that he and his followers could live as they had in the past. He refused to stay on a reservation. He hid out in mountains where the army could not find him. He refused to give up his freedom to come and go as he pleased. That made him a **renegade**. For years the army tried to capture Geronimo. They never did. He outsmarted and outran the **cavalry**.

Did you know?

American Indian **tribes** did not want to be ruled by the United States government. They already had their own governments and their own laws. The U.S. government forced American Indians to live on reservations so that they could not interfere with white settlers. Many reservations were far from the tribes' homelands.

Geronimo lived to be 80 years old.

How the man became a legend

Geronimo did kill many people, especially when he was on the run. But people blamed Geronimo for every act of American Indian violence, whether he was there or not. The newspapers printed many stories about Geronimo being "on the loose." Some were true, but many were not. These stories helped turn the man into a legend in his own lifetime. Geronimo's amazing ability to resist U.S. authorities and keep his freedom made him a symbol of the wild American West.

Geronimo did not start out as a freedom fighter. He lived a peaceful life. He had a wife and three young children. He also took care of his mother after his father died. Then, Mexican soldiers killed his entire family. They killed his children, his wife, and his mother. This tragedy left him aching for revenge.

Did you know?

U.S. paratroopers used to yell "Geronimo!" when they jumped out of airplanes during **World War II**. Private Aubrey Eberhardt was the first one to do it. He got the idea from the movies. He saw a Western about the U.S. cavalry fighting Geronimo. He yelled "Geronimo!" to show he was not afraid to jump. The custom spread through the paratroops. Later it even spread outside the army. Now people often yell "Geronimo!" when they do something daring.

FRANK LESLIE'S ILLUSTRATED NEWSPAPER

No. 1,618.—Vol. LXIII.] NEW YORK—FOR THE WEEK ENDING SEPTEMBER 25, 1886. [PRICE, 10 CENTS.

Pictures of Geronimo helped newspapers sell more copies.

Fact VS. Fiction

Myth: Geronimo was a chief.

Fact: Geronimo was the grandson of a chief, but he was never an Apache chief himself.

Who are the Apache?

The Apache are American Indians who used to live in Arizona and New Mexico. The word means "enemy" in another American Indian language. Geronimo's people did not use this name for themselves. Like many other American Indians, they called themselves simply "the people." Geronimo's group were the Bedonkohe, who were part of a larger **band** called the Chiricahuas.

The Gila River, in southeastern Arizona, was in the heart of Apache territory.

These Apache people posed in front of their **wickiups** near Camp Apache, Arizona, around 1870.

Trading and raiding

Geronimo's people were **nomads**. In summer they moved into the mountains where it was cool. In winter they went down to the river valleys where it was warmer. The land gave them most of what they needed. They found wild plants to eat. They hunted antelope and other **game** for food.

But there were things the land could not give, like horses, blankets, and guns. Apache people traded for these things. Sometimes they **raided** nearby Mexican villages and took what they needed. The Mexican government offered rewards for Apache **scalps**. This encouraged **bounty hunters** to kill as many American Indians as they could, including women and children.

Did you know?

The Spanish brought horses to North America in the 1500s. Before that no American Indian had ever seen or ridden a horse. But by the 1800s, many groups, including the Apache, were expert horsemen.

Young Geronimo

In his **autobiography**, Geronimo said he was born in 1829. But historians believe he was born in the early 1820s. Like his date of birth, the exact place where Geronimo was born is a mystery. It is likely that he was born by the Gila River, near the border of Arizona and New Mexico. There are many people who claim Geronimo was born in their town. But so far no one has found real proof.

Although his exact place of birth may be uncertain to historians, it is certain that Geronimo knew it well. His people believed that the place where a person was born was **sacred**. They returned to their place of birth throughout their life. Sometimes they performed **rituals** there for their health and well-being.

Apache babies were strapped to **cradleboards** and carried on their mother's back.

Did you know?

When Geronimo was born, the area where he lived was part of Mexico. After the Mexican-American War, in 1848, most of that land was given to the United States. Today it is part of Arizona and New Mexico. But Geronimo's people had lived there for many years. They believed the land belonged to them.

Did you know?

When Geronimo was in his eighties, in 1905 and 1906, he told his life story so that it could become part of the written history of the United States. A relative translated his words into English. Then the head of schools in Oklahoma wrote it down. Geronimo told his story the way he wanted. It is fascinating, but historians question how much of what he said was really true.

As a baby he was not given the name Geronimo. That warrior name came much later. His parents gave their new son the name Goyahkla, which means "one who yawns."

This Apache woman posed with her willow jugs and woven washbasins. Some Apache women still make traditional baskets just as their ancestors did hundreds of years ago.

Family

Geronimo was born into an important family. His father, Taklishim, was the son of Chief Mako of the Bedonkohe **band** of the Chiricahua Apache. Geronimo claimed he had seven brothers and sisters, but several of these were probably cousins. In the Chiricahua language, there is no difference between **siblings** and cousins. All are family. All are important.

Geronimo's mother, Juana, took care of him when he was a baby. Taklishim died when Geronimo was still a boy. Now it was his job to take care of his mother. Juana never married again.

Geronimo's family slept inside a **wickiup** similar to this one.

Fact VS. Fiction

Myth: All American Indians lived in **tipis.**

Fact: Geronimo's people lived in round homes called wickiups. These little houses were made of a frame of branches covered with long grass. They had a smoke hole in the middle of the roof and a door made of animal hide (skin).

This photo from 1886 shows Geronimo (on horseback) with his band of Chiricahua Apache warriors in the Sierra Madres.

War games

Apache children did not go to school at the time. Their games taught them important survival skills, such as how to hide. The Apache had many enemies, and there was always the danger of attack. Children who could hide were more likely to survive. And these skills would help later in life as well.

Boys learned to hunt. They played games where they threw and dodged rocks. They ran and trained hard to become warriors.

By age 17, Geronimo had gone on many **raids**. Now he was a man and could marry. He chose a girl named Alope, whom he loved very much.

Tragedy Strikes

In the 1850s, Geronimo took his family with him on a trading trip in Mexico. He had no idea that the Mexican Army was planning to attack the Apache. While he and most of the men were in town trading, Mexican troops stormed their camp. They killed and **scalped** almost everyone there. The dead included Geronimo's mother, wife, and three children.

Geronimo was heartbroken. In his **autobiography** he said, "I had no purpose left.... I had lost all." He went home and burned the **wickiup** where he had lived with his family. He burned all his wife's things and the children's toys. This was the Apache tradition.

From grief to power

In his grief, Geronimo went into the desert by himself. He later said that a voice suddenly spoke to him from out of nowhere. It called his name four times. Four is a magic number for the Apache. Geronimo knew something special was happening. The voice told him no gun would ever kill him. Geronimo knew he had been given power. His people believed that power came from their god. People with power could do amazing things.

Fact VS. Fiction

Myth: All American Indians scalped their enemies.

Fact: Scalping was brutal. The top of a person's head was sliced off with a knife. Some people survived scapling. Many did not. Scalping enemies was not an Apache tradition.

Pictures such as this one of Indian
violence increased fear and hatred
of Apache people among white settlers
in the 1800s.

Revenge!

Geronimo's heart ached for revenge. His chief sent him to meet with other Apache leaders. Geronimo asked them to help him get revenge on the Mexican soldiers who had killed his family. Chief Cochise of the Central Chiricahuas agreed. It took time to prepare. Then, almost a year after his family was killed, Geronimo finally led his people in revenge.

This was a war to kill, not a **raid**. They made camp outside the Mexican city of Arizpe. The Mexicans knew the Apache were there. Eight men came to try to make peace. But the Apache wanted blood, not words. They killed and scalped the Mexican men.

Cochise was a powerful Chiricahua. Like Geronimo, he became a fierce enemy of the Mexican Army after Mexican soldiers scalped his father.

This illustration shows Mexican soldiers around 1846 when the Mexican Army was at war with the United States.

Geronimo gets his new name

Finally the Mexican Army came out and fought. Geronimo got his warrior name in this bloody battle. It came from his enemies, the Mexicans. One legend says that he fought so fiercely that the Mexican soldiers cried out for Saint Jerome to save them. Geronimo is the Spanish name for "Jerome." The name stuck, and Geronimo's terrifying legend was born.

Did you know?

To the Apache people there was a big difference between raiding and going to war. Raids were for getting things the **tribe** needed, like horses and guns. Wars were for killing, not looting. Apache people only went to war when they believed they had been wronged. War was for revenge.

Thirst for Revenge

After that battle, most of the Apache were satisfied. But Geronimo was not. He continued to lead **raids** into Mexico. Geronimo trusted his power would protect him. But it did not protect those who fought by his side.

During an early morning raid on a Mexican town, Geronimo and two other warriors decided to steal some horses. Suddenly, gunfire exploded around them. The two other warriors were killed, and Geronimo ran for his life. The Mexicans chased him, but Geronimo knew how to hide. This skill saved his life. It took him days to get back home. And when he returned without the others, his people blamed him for their deaths.

A close call

Geronimo remarried. But he did not settle down to a peaceful family life like the one he had enjoyed with Alope and their children. Geronimo continued to seek revenge against his Mexican enemies.

In one raid, Geronimo slipped in a pool of blood. The butt of a gun slammed into his head. It knocked him out. When the battle was over, other Apache found him. They helped him back to camp. He carried the scar from that fight for the rest of his life. Geronimo later remembered the raid this way: "In this fight, we had lost so heavily that there really was no glory in our victory.... No one seemed to want to go on the war path again that year." No one but Geronimo.

Geronimo (right) posed for many photographs, including this one, after he surrendered in 1886.

The power

"No gun can ever kill you," the voice had said (see page 14). Geronimo was shot many times. His third finger was bent back from being struck by a bullet. He collected dozens of scars during his long and violent life. Some showed where knives and bullets had pierced his skin but failed to kill him.

His followers believed Geronimo had other powers too. They believed he could stop time. Once, when soldiers were chasing his raiding **band**, Geronimo's followers believed he delayed the dawn. The sun did not rise when it should have, so they were able to escape in darkness.

Because he believed he would not die in battle, Geronimo often behaved in reckless ways. This made life hard for his followers. He might have power, but they did not. Many died when he led them into danger. Other Chiricahuas suffered too. They were blamed for Geronimo's actions even when they had nothing to do with them.

Hide to survive

Geronimo also had an amazing ability to hide. He could become almost invisible. Once, when soldiers were chasing him through the mountains, he made himself blend into the rocks so well that the soldiers rode right past him.

Did you know?

The Apache people believe in one main spirit that gives power. This spirit is called Usen. **Medicine men** can use the power of Usen. When Geronimo got his power, he became a powerful medicine man.

This photograph of Apache dancers was taken around 1905. Some forms of dancing were and still are considered **sacred**.

A new enemy

Until the 1850s, Geronimo had no contact with the white settlers he would call White Eyes. The Mexicans were his enemy. But that began to change. Geronimo was already caught in a cycle of brutal revenge with the Mexicans. As more "White Eyes" came into Apache territory, they too would get caught up in this deadly tornado of violence.

Apache Pass and Fort Bowie

Settlers on their way to California went through the Apache Pass, in the heart of Apache country. American Indians attacked some of these **trespassers**. But that did not stop the flood of settlers. There were too many reasons for settlers to keep risking their lives to go west.

This U.S. troop was part of the 1886 campaign to capture Geronimo.

Fort Bowie was a base for the U.S. **Cavalry**. This photo was taken around 1885.

The U.S. government sent troops west to protect the settlers. In 1862 the government built Fort Bowie, hoping to use it as a base to control Apache Pass. Both the fort and the pass saw many bloody battles. Apache warriors would swoop down for an attack, then split up. Then the warriors would meet up somewhere else and attack again. The U.S. Army moved as a unit and could not chase them all down. Fort Bowie became even more famous as the site of the surrender of Geronimo in 1886.

The Apache Wars

Between 1851 and 1886, the Apache and White Eyes fought many battles. Geronimo had no grudge against the American settlers. The Mexicans were his sworn enemy, not the White Eyes. He did not hate them the way he hated Mexicans for the killing of his family. He actually liked the first white settlers he met.

But the white settlers were greedy. They wanted all the land, **game**, and water the Apache considered their own. The Apache needed things too. They continued to **raid**. Soon the Apache and White Eyes were at war.

An artist drew this picture in the 1880s. It shows Geronimo and his **band** returning from a raid in Mexico.

The "Cut Through the Tent" affair

In October 1860 some Apache men raided a settler's ranch. They stole animals and kidnapped the rancher's son. U.S. Army Lieutenant Nicholas Bascom was sent to get him back. Bascom wrongly believed the Chiricahuas were the kidnappers. He asked Chief Cochise to come talk to him at Apache Pass.

Cochise agreed and brought some tribesmen with him. He offered to help find the boy. Bascom thought Cochise was lying. He took the Apache men into a tent and told them they were prisoners. Cochise was furious. He cut a hole in the tent with his knife and escaped. But the other Apache men were still trapped inside. Cochise and his **tribe** captured some White Eyes. They offered to trade them for Cochise's people. Bascom refused. He killed all the Apache **hostages**. So Cochise killed the white hostages. This created a new cycle of deadly revenge.

White settlers built cabins like this one in Apache territory in the 1870s.

Family man...

Geronimo had several wives. This showed he was a good provider. Apache men could have more than one wife at a time only if they could provide for such a large family. Geronimo was devoted to his family, and his people continued to rely on him as a healer.

...or family killer?

Geronimo was not part of the "cut-through-the-tent" affair, but he was part of the revenge. He and his warriors rode from ranch to ranch, burning and killing. After a raid in the United States, he would race across the border into Mexico. He knew that the soldiers chasing him were not allowed to follow him into a different country. The U.S. Army gave orders to capture or kill Geronimo "at any cost."

A new weapon

Geronimo saw that U.S. soldiers had a new kind of gun—a rifle. It was far better than the old muskets that most Indians used. He attacked soldiers who had the new rifles. Then he took those weapons for himself and his warriors.

Did you know?

Rifles began to be used a lot in the 1840s and 1850s. Rifles are much more accurate than muskets. They have spiral grooves on the inside of the barrel. These grooves make the bullet spin as it comes out. A spinning bullet goes in a straighter path than one that doesn't spin.

This Apache scout is holding a rifle.

Battle of Apache Pass

By this time, Geronimo had joined the Warm Springs band, led by Chief Mangas Coloradas. In 1862 Cochise and Mangas Coloradas led 500 Apache warriors against U.S. soldiers at Apache Pass. The soldiers won. They fired **artillery** shells at the Apache. Mangas Coloradas was badly wounded in the battle.

Death of Chief Mangas Coloradas

Mangas Coloradas saw that the White Eyes had very powerful weapons. He feared his people would be wiped out if they did not make peace.

In 1863 he went alone to meet with General Joseph Rodman West at Fort McLane in New Mexico. West promised not to harm Mangas Coloradas. But the moment the chief was inside the fort, soldiers tortured and killed him.

African Americans in the U.S. Army were known as Buffalo Soldiers. Some fought in the Indian Wars against Geronimo and other Apache.

After he was dead, they cut off his head and boiled it. Then his skull was sent east to New York.

Once again Geronimo led Apache warriors in revenge. He terrorized white settlers. Geronimo was convinced that all White Eyes were liars and that Mangas Coloradas had been foolish to trust them. Geronimo would not make the same mistake.

Mangas Coloradas was chief of the Warm Springs Apache and one of Geronimo's uncles through marriage.

Chief Mangas Coloradas

(about 1795–1863)

Mangas Coloradas lived from about 1795 to 1863. He was known as a fierce warrior who hated white Americans. But he was also a wise leader who tried to do what was right for his people. Some historians say he was the greatest Apache leader of all.

Camp Grant Massacre

Camp Grant was a military base in southern Arizona. It was named after Ulysses S. Grant, who was president of the United States at that time. In 1871 a young army officer, Royal Whitman, took command. Whitman was friendly to the Apache people. He gave them food and blankets. Soon hundreds of Apache people came to live on the land near the camp. They farmed and lived peacefully with the white settlers.

But other Apache people in the area were still attacking settlers. An angry mob from the nearby frontier town of Tucson, Arizona, attacked the Apache people who had settled at Camp Grant. They had enlisted the help of Papago American Indians. The Papago were bitter enemies of the Apache. They attacked at a time when most of the men were out hunting and killed about 144 Apache, mostly women and children. They also kidnapped 28 or 29 Apache children and sold them into slavery in Mexico.

Massacre or murder?

Newspapers called the attack a **massacre**. President Grant called it murder. He ordered a criminal trial. But most of the jury was made up of Arizona settlers. They hated all Apache people. They didn't care whether some were peaceful or not. They wanted them all dead. So the jury found the accused not guilty. They were free to go, and the kidnapped Apache children were never returned.

Ulysses S. Grant was the 18th president of the United States.

Apache Pass Reservation

In 1872 Chief Cochise finally agreed to put the Chiricahuas on a **reservation**. He believed this would save his people. The government gave them 3,000 square miles (7,700 square kilometers) of land. It included their homeland near Apache Pass.

Geronimo went to this reservation with his family. The white settlers hoped that now the Apache **raids** would stop. After all, the Apache people had their land. And the government gave them food and blankets.

But Geronimo did not change his way of life. He still went on raids. Most of them took him across the border into Mexico. Then he returned to the reservation. Sometimes he brought herds of stolen cattle with him. The Mexican government complained to the U.S. government. It was a tense situation.

In 1874 Cochise died. After his death, the U.S. government moved the Chiricahuas north to a new reservation.

San Carlos Reservation

The San Carlos Reservation was nothing like the mountains the Apache people loved. The land was flat and hot. There were scorpions and rattlesnakes. Mosquitoes bred in the rivers and carried diseases. And many different Apache **tribes** had to live together. This was not their way. No one liked living there.

Geronimo said he would go to San Carlos. But instead he fled with about 700 of his people. He took them into the mountains of Mexico.

Apache people were forced to dig ditches at the San Carlos Reservation. This was part of the U.S. government's plan to turn them into farmers.

The next 10 years

Geronimo used the Sierra Madre Mountains as a base. From there he led warriors on raids into Arizona.

John Clum (see box) was the government agent in charge of San Carlos. He was determined to catch Geronimo. In 1877 Clum set a trap. He heard that Geronimo was going to visit the Warm Springs Reservation. Clum took 80 armed American Indian police with him.

When they got there, the American Indian police hid so that Geronimo would not see them when he arrived. Geronimo came to talk to Clum. He was not afraid. Then Clum gave the signal. The American Indian police jumped out with their guns pointed at Geronimo. Clum took Geronimo to San Carlos in chains. His plan was to hang the war leader as a murderer.

But a new agent replaced Clum before he could hang Geronimo. Geronimo was released, and he broke out of the reservation again. Over the next few years, Geronimo lived on the run. Sometimes he would return to the reservation and "surrender." But he never settled down. He raided and killed white settlers and Mexicans. His reputation grew. Whenever a stagecoach was robbed, people said, "Geronimo did it!" Sometimes he did, but often he did not.

John Philip Clum

(1851–1932)

John Clum (pictured center) grew up in New York State. He came west in his early twenties to run the San Carlos Reservation. Clum tried to be fair. But he wanted Apache people to live like farmers. Some Apache people respected him. Others hated him.

Surrender at Skeleton Canyon

General Crook (see box) and his American Indian scouts tracked Geronimo for 10 months. In early 1886 they found him in Mexico. Geronimo was in his sixties. He was still strong, but his followers were exhausted. For their sakes, Geronimo gave up. He said, "Once I moved around like the wind and now I surrender. That is all." But on the way back to San Carlos, he and some other Apache escaped again.

This photo was taken soon after Geronimo (left) surrendered to General Crook (right) in Tombstone, Arizona.

General George Crook

(1828–1890)

General Crook was commander of the Arizona Territory during part of the Apache Wars. The Apache people nicknamed him Gray Wolf because he was such a strong, tough opponent.

The U.S. government was furious. It sent General Nelson Miles to replace Crook. For five months, 5,000 U.S. soldiers, led by General Miles, chased Geronimo. It was the largest military campaign in U.S. history. And the enemy was one man: Geronimo.

The last surrender

The soldiers never caught him. American Indian scouts were the only ones who could find Geronimo. They walked bravely into his camp. Geronimo wanted to kill them. The other Chiricahuas would not let him. The scouts were family. Geronimo saw that he had no friends anymore. His own people were helping his enemies. On September 4, 1886, Geronimo gave himself up at a place called Skeleton Canyon. The Apache Wars were over.

General George Crook (on horseback) needed Apache scouts (left and right) to find Geronimo.

Far from home

Geronimo and all the Chiricahuas—even the scouts—became **prisoners of war**. They were put on a train to Florida. Geronimo never saw his homeland again.

On the way to Florida, the train stopped in Texas. President Grover Cleveland wanted Geronimo hanged. But General Miles stepped in. He argued that Geronimo was a prisoner of war and they must honor the agreement not to execute him. This probably saved Geronimo's life.

Geronimo picked melons and other vegetables with his family at their farm on the **reservation** at Fort Sill, Oklahoma.

The Chiricahuas continued to Florida. Life there was even worse than at San Carlos. Diseases ran through the crowded camps. The Chiricahuas could not find the healing herbs and plants they knew. Many died. Most blamed Geronimo for what had happened to them.

In 1894 the government moved the Chiricahuas to Fort Sill in Oklahoma. Their new home there was much better. It was more like what they were used to than Florida.

Celebrity

With no wars, Geronimo was no longer a war leader. His people did not regard him as a hero. But the white Americans could not get enough of Geronimo. Geronimo became an **entrepreneur**. He sold the buttons off his coat. He sold his autograph. Other American Indians gave him beadwork to sell. Anything he touched was worth money to white Americans who were hungry for a **souvenir**.

Geronimo appeared at the World's Fair in 1904. In 1905 he rode in President Theodore Roosevelt's **inaugural** parade. After the parade, Geronimo begged the new president to let him go home to Arizona. He wanted to die there. But the president refused, so Geronimo returned to Fort Sill.

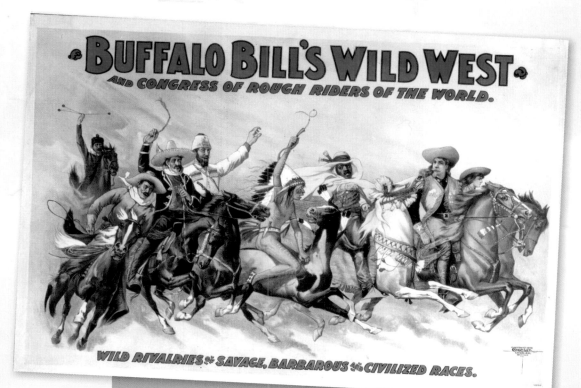

Geronimo appeared in Buffalo Bill's Wild West show.

In the end even Geronimo had regrets. "I should never have surrendered," he whispered on his deathbed. "I should have fought until I was the last man alive."

This grave in Fort Sill, Oklahoma, is where Geronimo and other Indians are buried.

The death of Geronimo

Although he remained a prisoner of war until his death, Geronimo was not locked up in a jail. He was an old man, in his eighties. Sometimes he rode into town. In February 1909, on his way back from town, Geronimo fell off his horse. He lay in a cold, wet ditch all night long. By the time someone found him, he was sick. A few days later, on February 17, Geronimo died.

What Geronimo means today

White settlers thought Geronimo was the fiercest Apache warrior anyone had ever seen. He was a monster who killed defenseless children. But he was also the victim of that same violence against his own family.

Even his own people do not agree about this man who became a legend. Some believe he was a proud freedom fighter. Others think his endless quest for revenge was selfish. He made a difficult life even more difficult for his people.

When the Apache Wars ended, people no longer feared Geronimo. As more years passed, people learned that the American Indians were very badly treated. Geronimo became a symbol of the untamed West. Some still think of him as a hero.

Timeline

1823
This was probably the year Geronimo was born, although he gives the date as 1829.

1846
Geronimo marries his first wife, Alope.

1846-1848
War takes place between Mexico and the United States.

1850
The Territory of New Mexico is established (which included the present-day states of New Mexico, Arizona, and southern Colorado).

1852
Geronimo and combined forces of different tribes wipe out Mexican soldiers to avenge the deaths of his family and others killed the year before. This is also when he gets his warrior name Geronimo.

1851
This was probably the year Geronimo's family was killed by Mexican soldiers, although he gives the year as 1858. Soon after, he is said to be given the gift of power: He cannot be killed in battle.

1855
Warm Springs Reservation is established.

1861
"Cut Through the Tent" Affair occurs.

1863
Mangas Coloradas is tortured and killed by soldiers.

1874
Cochise dies.

1877
Clum captures Geronimo at Warm Springs Reservation and takes him to San Carlos in chains.

1885
Geronimo leads about 100 Apache from San Carlos to Mexico. On the way they kill 17 settlers.

1884
Geronimo surrenders to General Crook and returns to San Carlos Reservation.

1877
Warm Springs Reservation is closed and the Apache are moved to San Carlos.

1886
Geronimo surrenders to Crook (some of the famous photos of him are taken at this time) then runs off again. General Miles replaces Crook. Scouts find Geronimo and persuade him to surrender. Geronimo surrenders to Miles. Apache prisoners of war are shipped to Florida.

1894
The surviving Apache are shipped to Fort Sill.

1909
Geronimo dies at Fort Sill, Oklahoma.

1905
Geronimo rides in President Theodore Roosevelt's inaugural parade. He tells his life story to S. M. Barrett, who writes *Geronimo: His Own Story*.

1904
Geronimo appears at the World's Fair in St. Louis, Missouri.

Family Tree

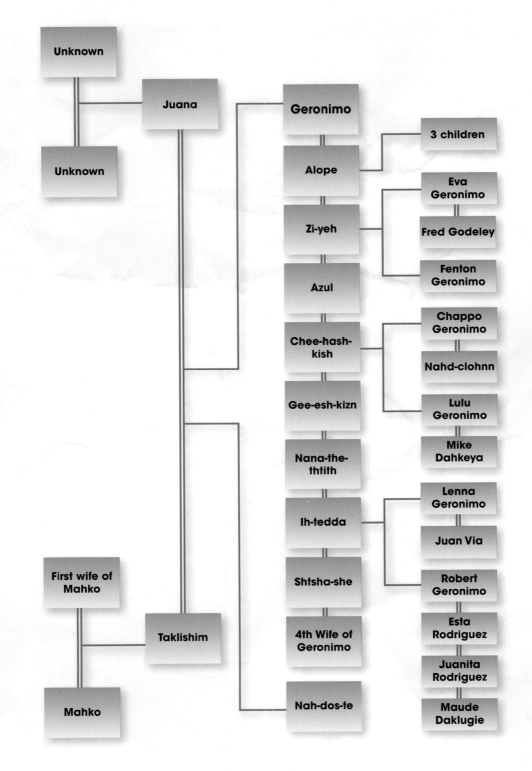

Unknown

Juana

Geronimo

Unknown

Alope — 3 children

Zi-yeh — Eva Geronimo

Fred Godeley

Azul — Fenton Geronimo

Chee-hash-kish — Chappo Geronimo

Nahd-clohnn

Gee-esh-kizn — Lulu Geronimo

Mike Dahkeya

Nana-the-thtith

Ih-tedda — Lenna Geronimo

Juan Via

Shtsha-she — Robert Geronimo

First wife of Mahko

Taklishim

4th Wife of Geronimo — Esta Rodriguez

Juanita Rodriguez

Mahko

Nah-dos-te — Maude Daklugie

Glossary

artillery
large guns, such as cannons

autobiography
published story of one's own life, written by the subject of the book

band
group of American Indians that lives together like an extended family

bounty hunter
person who goes after other people for a reward

cavalry
part of an army that fought on horses

cradleboard
wooden frame used by American Indian women for carrying an infant

entrepreneur
businessperson

game
type of animal that can be hunted for food

hostage
prisoner held in order to be traded for something, such as for a group's own prisoners

inaugural
marking a beginning

massacre
brutal killing of many people at once

medicine man
healer with supernatural powers

nomad
person who moves from place to place with no permanent home

prisoner of war (POW)
soldier caught by the enemy during a war and kept as a prisoner

raid
attack to steal horses and supplies; to carry out such an attack

renegade
traitor or rebel

reservation
land set aside by the government for a special purpose, such as a place for American Indians to live

ritual
religious ceremony where people use symbols to express their cultural heritage

sacred
holy

scalp
top part of the head where hair grows; to cut off and take this part

sibling
brother or sister

souvenir
something bought or kept as a reminder of someone or an important event

tipi
cone-shaped shelter made of poles and animals hides

trespasser
person on land that belongs to someone else

tribe
group that shares a common purpose, language, and culture

wickiup
round hut

World War II
war fought from 1939 to 1945 that involved all of the world's major powers

Find Out More

Books

Feinstein, Stephen. *Read About Geronimo (I Like Biographies!).* Berkeley Heights, N.J.: Enslow, 2006.

Haugen, Brenda. *Geronimo: Apache Warrior (Signature Lives).* Mankato, Minn.: Compass Books, 2006.

Sterngass, Jon. *Geronimo (Legends of the Wild West).* New York: Chelsea House, 2010.

Sullivan, George. *Geronimo: Apache Renegade.* New York: Sterling Biographies, 2010.

DVDs

American Experience: Geronimo and the Apache Resistance. Directed by Neil Goodwin and Jacqueline Shearer. PBS, 2007.

Biography: Geronimo. A&E Home Video, 2006.

"Geronimo," American Experience: We Shall Remain. Narrated by Benjamin Bratt. PBS Home Video, 2009.

Native American Wars: The Apache. A&E Home Video, 2010.

Wild West Tech: Native American Tech. A&E Television Networks, 2008.

Websites

Chiricahua Apache Prisoners of War
http://blog.nmai.si.edu/main/2011/02/telling-it-the-right-way-chiricahua-apache-prisoners-of-war.html
Here you'll find a documentary of the Chiricahua prisoners of war as told by members of the tribe.

Smithsonian National Museum of the American Indian
www.nmai.si.edu/
Find information about the American Indians, including the Apache and Chiricahua and find pictures of Geronimo.

A Song for the Horse Nation: Horses in Native American Cultures
http://americanindian.si.edu/exhibitions/horsenation/guns.html
This website discusses the impact of the horse on American Indian cultures. You can also see a picture of Geronimo and the common rifles used in his lifetime.

"Too Long a Way Home: Healing Journey of the Chiricahua Apaches"
http://blog.nmai.si.edu/main/2011/05/too-long-a-way-home-healing-journey-of-the-chiricahua-apaches.html
Historian Mark Hirsch talks about the life of Geronimo in this article from American Indian magazine.

Places to visit

George Gustav Heye Center of the National Museum of the American Indian
Alexander Hamilton U.S. Custom House
One Bowling Green
New York, NY 10004
212-514-3700
www.nmai.si.edu/subpage.cfm?subpage=visitor&second=ny

Geronimo Trail National Scenic Byway
211 Main Street
Truth or Consequences, NM 87901
575-894-1968
www.geronimotrail.com/

Gila National Forest
3005 East Camino del Bosque
Silver City, NM 88061
575-388-8201
http://fs.usda.gov/gila/

Fort Sill National Historic Landmark Museum
437 Quanah Road
Fort Sill, OK 73503
580-442-5123
http://sill-www.army.mil/museum/visit.htm

Index